THE
PAINTED BUNTING'S
LAST MOLT

PITT POETRY SERIES

ED OCHESTER, EDITOR

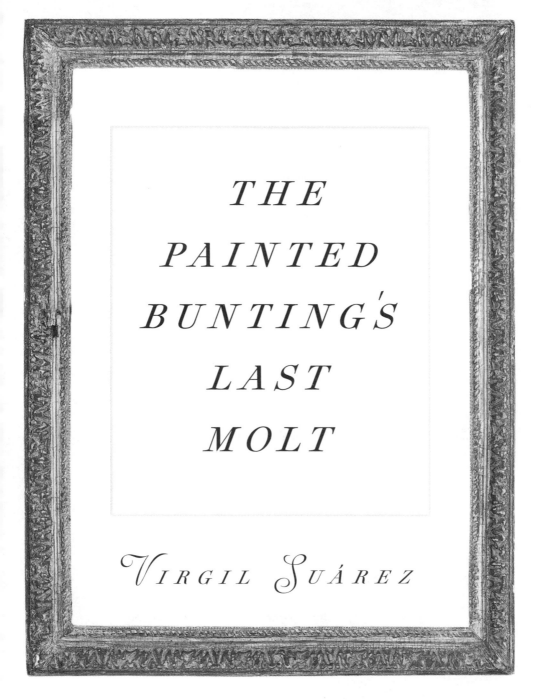

THE PAINTED BUNTING'S LAST MOLT

VIRGIL SUÁREZ

UNIVERSITY OF PITTSBURGH PRESS

Published by the University of Pittsburgh Press, Pittsburgh, Pa., 15260
Manufactured in the United States of America
Printed on acid-free paper
10 9 8 7 6 5 4 3 2 1

ISBN 13: 978-0-8229-6609-8
ISBN 10: 0-8229-6609-3

Cover art: *Der gemahlte Ammer* from Johann Wolf, *Abbildungen und Beschreibungen merkwürdiger naturgeschichtlicher Gegenstände, 1818–1822*. Atlas. Field Museum of Natural History Library
Cover design: Joel W. Coggins

For My Mother

&

All the Suárez-Poey Children

&

Ed Ochester, poeta y editor del alma

CONTENTS

PART III: EXEGESIS

PART IV: HYPERGRAPHIA

The children observe
a point far, far away.
   —**Federico García Lorca**

THE
PAINTED BUNTING'S
LAST MOLT

PART I

INDIGO

Lament for the Boy Rafter

Every day on his way to school he stops briefly to smell
        the sea air, look askance toward the horizon,

stare at the wind-swept coconut palm fronds, their shimmer
        of light, and on his way home to the clapboard, makeshift

hut, he studies the cracks on the dusty earth, counts pebbles,
        picks up twigs, and combs his fingers through scrub grass.

He reads the infected mosquito scabs on his arms, walks home
        daydreaming of how wood floats on water.

He tells his father, his mother, his friends
        not to wait up for him if one day he does not return.

They laugh at him, this skinny boy of nine, green
        eyes, green spirit, and at night, in the waking of things lost,

he dreams of buoyancy, splintered pieces of wood, an inner tube,
        black circles on the water, all line up from Santiago to Miami,

and he skips across one inner tube to another on his way North.

Mirage

> When the low, heavy sky weighs like the giant lid
> of a great pot upon the spirit crushed by care,
> and from the whole horizon encircling us is shed
> a day blacker than night, and thicker with despair.
>   —**Charles Baudelaire**

Here on the high seas, the ocean is possessed
of a thousand hues between lapis lazuli and indigo,
and on this north bound rinky-dink raft, another
family prays to Yemaya, Holy Mother of the Crossing,

to spare the lives of everyone on board.
But is it too late? The sun has blistered the skin,
ravaged the skin of old leprous San Lazaro
who dizzy stumbles overboard into the water,

disappears into the darkness, and now not even
with burnt offerings will the sea return him, a kiss
of night and air on the full moon, the children
have stopped crying, the only sound left is breath

upon a parched tongue, those who say the sea
is the great mother are liars, it is the great void.
By morning even the storm clouds dissipate,
a welcoming sign of calm and peace, the horizon

undulates, sea birds scattershot into the heavens.

Mother Under Water

She learns to stay down for good,
        water fills her ears with voices.
        They speak of this riddle of waves,
of so much plummeting,

her eyes darken, her hands reach
        for shadows, claw at them,
        become anemones in the shade
of this half-lit dream. Her efforts to push

her son along leaves her exhausted.
        In her lungs, the water heavy
        like mercury. Her fever dreams

of her precious cargo crush the night.
Underneath him she continues to drag
toward the shore, her body a ghostly
vessel nobody will witness in the depths.

When Leaving the Country of Your Birth

Will the wind remember your body, its weight
        slanted against a white wall?

Will the river flood the valleys, carve a new path
        into the roots of mountains?

Will palm trees bend and birth coconuts,
        these yellow beacons in the blinding light?

Will buildings crumble into rubble and dust,
        ruins of memory's instant flash?

Will your aunt's parrot still hang by the doorway
        that leads to the patio, calling out, "*Mariposa!*"

Will the sea rush El Malecón in dangerous weather?

Will your old house stand in the shadows
        of all the plantains your father planted?

Will the baobab at the corner grow wider, it's elephant
        skin roots sunk deep into the earth?

Who will remember you, child? Who will sigh
        your name?

Who will greet you there in the old neighborhood
        upon your return?

Who will say that you are now a "*mariposa*," not
        a "*gusano*"?

Who will trace the bread crumbs this far out?

Blue Cuban

Is it her apparition in water?
This distance between two points
That clutches memory by the throat?

The way a speck of land, a peak
rises in the horizon, looms like wreckage.
Palm fronds sifted by winds.

Clouds bunched up over thatch roofs,
a sleek rain falling over banyans,
jacarandas and baobabs.

Is it the perfect orb of mangoes?
Soursop and papaya aroma?
When the flock of feral parrots

screech by, the dread of eternal
exile roots itself in water. Is it the poet's
song, Lorca's moment of despair,

the sound of one bata drum,
the *che-che* of chekeres? Women
dressed in white in demonstrations.

Everyone returns to water in time.
Whoever dares conjure this blueness
cannot help but surrender to it.

The Art of Raft Making

This is how you become intimate with the tincture
　　　　　of sky that hurts the eyes, the way skin turns
pale after two days of floating—tiny creatures seek

solace in your hair, armpits, loins in particular,
　　　　　that concave of shadow, respite from the sun.
At night, other than the star-pocked sky,

there is little difference between the slicked surface
　　　　　of the water and the heavens. A moon recoils
from its own ghostly phosphorescence. What does

the sea remember of the pull of an oar? It's swath?
　　　　　The path of a homemade raft? A body
adrift in eternal supplication. The sun wreaks havoc

on the skin, swelters, sizzles into button-sized
　　　　　callouses. Fish learn to nibble and dash,
until nothing is left but this incessant fantasy

of floating. When the sea and night become accomplices
　　　　　this silent history of absence in the eyes
of the unseen, unheard from, scan the horizon for tell-

tale signs, when your eyes sting from searching so hard.

Balsero / **Rafter**

What lures you to the lip of water
so dark in the night? Starglow, riddles

of moonlight, silken and indifferent,
this churning of endless waves,

warm water, currents that take you
always North towards tomorrow?

Inner tubes, rope, plastic milk jugs,
the kind tourists throw out car windows.

In them one hundred *cucuyos*, fireflies,
their green luminescence a needed light

to illuminate the way on such dark nights.
Listen carefully to the language of water.

Two bodies can fit on a slab of styrofoam,
keep warm in the southerly breeze—teeth

chatter or is it the maracas enunciating
the names of all the dead *balseros*?

Who braved the currents but did not beat
the odds? A worm moon blushes white?

An absent witness to such bitter crossings.

Moon Decima

If it were the Eucharist, it'd be hard to swallow,
this moon of lost impressions, a boy in deep water,
something tickling his skin. This memory of weight-
lessness—a kite that somehow still manages to hover
in the dog mouth blackness of sky. This is a cut out
moon of lost children, or is it a savior's moon?
This boy will float on home, or be swallowed
by the water. Above the pines and mangroves,
this moon hangs unrelenting. Is it the one eye
of an indifferent God that remains open just so?

Caribbean Catechism

This is how you swim further, faster,
        keep you eyes on the water,
flail your arms, then warm up,

slice through like oars, so sure,
        rhythmic, the way north assured.
What I like about water is it knows

how to keep a secret. A body slices
        through without leaving a trace,
when you must leave in the night.

The night too has learned
        To keep its mouth shut.
When you speak of sin and repentance,

The Eucharist fills your mouth
        so completely it looks
like you are gasping for air,

your water-logged lungs become
        the necessary sinkers,
luring you down into darker depths.

After Kcho's *La columna infinita*

Inspired by Constantin Brancusi's *Endless Column*

All wood drowns . . . soaks up water,
right there in its softened core, right there
where the human hand grips, a fingernail
sinks into it in its desire to stay afloat.

How much wood? How many hands?
The sea never tallies. There is no score.
Like an old house that takes all the wood
you offer. With its blackened underbelly,

with its dagger-slit eyes. *Toda madre se unde*,
submerges, goes under long enough to spell
out this secret longing for wetness. This enigma
of those who plunge into the sea on a wooden

raft. Most perish, some live to drift ashore.
"Nothing changes," the artist claims,
"and everything does. Nothing is constant."
Except for a piece of wood, this plank here,

a broken oar, floating like an open embrace.

Hot House

My maternal grandparents' house in San Pablo,
Cuba, didn't have air conditioning so in summer,
right before the rains, my father couldn't sleep.

At night the asthmatic stayed up cursing, walking
about in his underwear, no shirt on, his skin
glistening with sweat. He sat in the darkened

kitchen and fanned himself with an old *Granma*,
and I could hear his feet against the hard-packed
dirt floor of Abuela Tina's kitchen. "*Que calor!*"

The heat lapped at my face. Sometimes I rose
and joined him by the door of the kitchen,
and we looked out at the paleness of the moon,

and in the distance the fireflies flashed in the grass,
and the wild dogs whimpered, bats rustled wings
up in the almond trees. All creatures restless

in the heat. Hot house, my grandfather said,
and we were all wilting orchids, these midnight
flowers that chose to bloom, then suffer heat.

Arabesques

Sunlight's knife slices through banana plant fronds,
my grandmother's insistence on cutting out shapes

from gold leaf paper, glued them to the back of books,
called them spirit-shadows, of long veil-tailed gold fish,

egrets of magnificent plumage, holy places like the Taj
Mahal, Bengal tigers in the throes of shade, respite,

its hunger appeased by the life of a wild boar, a man
his wife, their only son, two suitcases, the impermanence

of light entering her bedroom where she'd die speaking
the names of her own parents whom she said emerged

from a shaft of light and reached out to her, and I put out
my hand between my grandmother and the light,

felt nothing, perhaps a slight warmth, then I saw them,
the tiny gold flecks catching the light just so, corpuscles

of the unseen. I held my breath and wanted to believe
that through light, through its sharp brightness and contrast

against a bedroom tile floor, two bodies can say goodbye,
one fallen silent, the other stirred on this day and later

that night when from inside one of the books, a ribbon
of golden paper unfolds like the tongue of ages, spitting

tiny people holding hands, going out beyond the mattress,
the room, out the door and into the darkness, then toward light.

Liminality

The summer of the great floods
      when my father, the gravedigger
worked at the Colon Cemetery,
      he came home one day to tell
my mother the coffins floated away,
      emerged from water-swollen
earth to move into rip-roaring
      street floods, some broke
open, cadavers bobbed and sunk
      on the pudding-sludge water.
After the dead, came the bloated
      dogs, goats, chickens.
There went dictators, poets, thieves—
      Smiles fixed on their bleached
faces. Clumps of dead hair swirled
      in the slow current.
I stood by the window a saw empty
      streets. In the bathroom my
father's rubber boots stood in a corner,
      limp like appendages, caked
with black mud. I thought about
      the nature of lines, what keeps
truth from lies, a fresh-dug grave
      my father stood inside to shovel.
I rubbed a dab of mud between fingers,
      Sniffed at it for traces of the dead.
I thought of bodies floating toward
      the ocean, congregating
in the mouths of sewers, their arms twisted
      hooked up as if in a dance,
nobody wanting to let go of each other.

Vibrational Reciprocity

Doug Anderson, a poet I admire brings
to my attention the Coconut Monk,

"who lived on a floating island on the Mekong
with a huge statue of the Buddha on one end

and another huge statue of Jesus on the other."
Whose followers included American service men

who went AWOL during the war and to whom
the monk, being a pacifist, provided refuge.

I am reading about the Coconut Monk during
a graduate student's defense in musicology:

something about how vibrational resonance
affects the human voice, the *Duende's* blues .

I am 8 years old, I am standing by a huge 55 gallon
drum my father placed in the corner of the patio

to collect rain water so my mother could do
the laundry and wash the dishes. The storms

have passed. Drops fall into the filled drum.
Havana, Cuba 1970, Cuban military advisors

fighting on the side of the North Vietnamese.
One drop at a time. One plops in and waves ripple

to the brim and return to the center. I see
a boat on a river carrying the remains of pacifists

who died waiting for that war and many others
to end. I see a man on a balcony get shot,

another on the floor of a California hotel kitchen
bleeding out, a man whispering not to let

go into his ear. Another drop. Like this poem
rippling into the world expecting something in return.

PART II

THE

PAINTED

BUNTING

Caribbean Dreams Lexicon

My grandmother drank espresso out of a cut gourd,
and she would say she loved the taste of sweetened coffee
in it. Me, the child, perched on her lap looking into a mirror.

In the mirror, my parents are waving at me, they smile
to check their teeth, they are headed to a funeral.
My grandmother says they will return because they miss

their concave lives, and each night, before she puts me to sleep,
she sings a prayer for the worn, the lost, for the unremembered,
how each night, my grandmother thought she could hear

the ghostly echoes of the rain falling, taking us back to Manhattan
where she spent her early years with her father, the engineer,
working on the bridge. She has forgotten how to speak English

but she tells this story of how some travel far away only to return,
still refugees in their own countries. We live in countries
we cannot possibly die in, she says, and blows out the light.

Homing

Last night on the Discovery Channel
scientists discussed how some birds,
frigate birds, pelicans, albatross use

magnetic fields as a way to orient
themselves toward the North, a red
dot (a simulation on screen), I guess.

They see this red dot that guides
them in their retinas, or in the corners
of their wide-eye awe. And I think

of the woman my parents befriended
in Spain, Eloisa—who cried all day
and all night, and my parents didn't

know how to console her, or what
needed to be done because she said
she was homesick, no way for her

to return to Cuba. This was 1970,
and Eloisa spoke through her crying,
a mouth and throat full of saliva,

a lost drowning woman. In her eyes,
the one time she held me, I saw
this world of directionless blue water,

dark indigo worlds of the lost.
Eloisa's eyes became those red dots,
her exiled darkness rising behind me

to disorient me, render me silent.

Caribe

All colors pale in its waters,
      white becomes bone,
      the rock that sinks you,

what chances, fateful nights
      for those who succumb to this allure
      of water, as it calls you out

to swim away into its currents,
      this restlessness of days,
      teeth chatter, a clatter

of broken promises behind,
      the Siboney knew a thousand
      words for the essence of water,

mud eyes, clay mouths,
      fatal hours when the spirit
      leaves the body to join a starless

night, when all you have
      are questions, look to water
      for the flickering answers.

Havana Blue

This city will always need work, hands upon it,
calloused, a sheet of sandpaper to scratch its own
back, what my mother calls *el desrumbe*, flecks
of paint everywhere, a riddle for the ashen pigeons.

This city will always need old men, children
in uniform, a knot of banyan tendrils at the park,
a white-wash glare, broken glass, windows agape
like the mouths of its citizens. Music fills empty

spaces, dead hours blue with boredom. Cheap rum
scented hallways, porticos, a bricolage of grid-iron.
The sea keeps this secret of blanched sky, birds
soar for morsels. A litany of rumors, a clatter

of jackhammers in the moonlight. Slacked days,
and ebb, a tug to plunder, what the carpenters know
of wood, a termite's solemnity in dank crevices,
pockets of chiaroscuro. This city will always

stand erect, no matter its conquered history.
A man can either aim for the moon, or canoe
across its bay to cast empty nets. Questions
are for restless spirits, answers for those drowning.

Blue Line

A perfect morning in Key Biscayne
is not rare, but you have to rise
      early to catch it, a hue so blue

it hurts the eyes hovers above the coast line,
light fills everything with blinding
      splendor—water sprinklers snap-hissing

on to condominium lawns
& walkways—this constant susurrus
      of innuendoes.

If you sit quiet and still long enough,
you can hear carp gobble up
      the edges of the lotus plants.

A dragonfly's wings chatter on a reed.
A moment's respite, for sure.
      In the distance, a sailboat pushes

against the shifting horizon, a gloved
hand, a flower bloom, a single cloud,
      a plume floats by—what is written

there on the sky is for everyone
to read. Moments like this, so perfect,
      gorged with fragility beyond horizons.

A History of Rain

There's something mind-numbing about waking
        up to rain on a Monday afternoon, its drip-drip
filtering in through the open-slatted windows.

I remember rainy school days in Cuba
        when I watched its patterns on the walls,
hear its rushing down the street. My parents

took me. I dreaded the soggy earth.
        Gang boys' harassment enough, and now rain.
I hated the rain's mocking fall, its sounds,

its slickness on the streets, light blurring
        on the windshields of cars. I have thought
of blue dying, a terrible melancholia gripping

the spirit. I remember my hatred of wet. Frogs
        in Havana ready to croak from some dark V
of a plantain frond. The unexpected, a skidding

of tires. I hear it now, beyond my study,
        children kept in cages on the Border,
no parents in sight and the overhead fluorescent light

humming. It is a negative power that clutches
        you by the throat. Death pants in the sound
of the rain. You hear it too?

La sangre llama

A flash-flicker of light on the back of a leaf,
when one carp gobbles up air on a pond's surface,
bubbles pop, small ripples form, in my hands
the hardness of pebbles, a rock in the chest
when bad news comes from the Sick Island,
isla enferma, the only one I care about,
a lover's map of nostalgia, how penumbra
and solitude whip themselves into a *frenesi*
of longing for what can never be, must not be
remembered, how the child walks back each
day from school, from church, a song
of the lost on his lips—what lasts here?
Bliss of *exilio*, a man who can never find his way
back. The sight of water makes him dizzy,
reminds him of the people who have followed
him here through so much water and melancholy,
to this place where blood refuses to forget the names.

After Lorca's "The Ballad of the Sleepwalker"

In this damp world of the tropics, seen by your own
       eyes, verdigris is precisely the color. Where water
ebbs and flows over river rock, worn smooth, flushed

       with the patina of lichen, mossy tuffs kissed in cracks.
The palm trees are regal in their new dress of fronds.
       Okay, *verde* like its inedible *cocos*. A snapping turtle

suns on a half-submerged log, its head an arrow, still
       under its heavy, duckweed-veiled carapace. Who
would mistake it for a rock? This radiant panorama

       is what must have driven the crew in Columbus' ships
to dive in and swim ashore. The history of their journey
       frothing in their mouths. Call it green surrender.

Jaibas

The Cubans on Key Biscayne
call them *jaibas*, these blueish

crabs that appear en masse
on the steamy roads, between

the medians, under the beige
tendril roots of the mighty

banyans, by the coconut palms—
they invade the key on a mating-

eating spree once a year—such
urgency in their scuttling ways

to be squashed by cars, they stink
up the place. One day here,

gone the next. Beachcombers
fill buckets with them, take

them home to boil and feast.
The crabs simply want to cross

from one end of the shore
to the other, find a mate.

How can the Cubans not
be jealous. Unlike the *jaibas*

their own water crossings
have never been this easy

nor this blue and portentous.

Days of Ornithology

My cousin and I traveled into the woods
on horseback to catch birds in our traps,
*tomeguines, mariposas, sinsonte*s, or, if lucky,
an *azulejo*, this bird whose powder blue
flashed like thunder between branches,
and my cousin rode determined to catch
one or a pair. He said that bird sang unlike
any other, better than the canaries my
uncle kept in endless cages and bred them.
Previously we'd caught *tomeguines* which
make nests in low shrubs, making it easy
to sneak up behind them, cup the entrance
to the nest and trap an entire family.

But, the *azulejo* only came to Cuba to molt,
to change into its iridescent plumage
for mating season, and we often stopped long
enough while the horse drank at a pool's edge
to hear its call from the periphery of the forest,
there it sat on the branches of Jacarandas
to preen new feathers and warble for a mate.
We hurried toward it, each time fooled
by this swift bird, as if it knew our purpose,
this hide-and-seek game became the lure
of that which kept my cousin and I's dreams
from ending, at least not this summer, nor
the next, our need for blue words, blue longing.

My Mother's Mouth Fills with Water

Gallop of horses on the roof,
          my daughters say, when this
storm starts up, relentless, over
          night. Water rushes
out toward the slope of land,
          runs into ponds, ravines,
fills those gulches tracked on dirt
          by the heavy garbage
and UPS delivery trucks, frogs finally
          silent in these downpours.
I stay up into the early morning hours,
          counting the claps of thunder,
flashes of lightning. I think of the salesman
          at the funeral home in Hialeah
where my mother died, and how
          he proposed the extra rubber
seal for the casket, an added
          expense, "you know how water
gets into everything in Florida," he
          said. And I think of my mother
drowning below the earth; how
          fitting for an islander to return
to water, to return home whichever
          way possible. Blessed water
that carries us deeper than we intend to go.

Monsoon

The villagers are never caught unprepared,
        they know how to detect the early warnings,
breaking open of sky, cloud, and rain pours
incessantly from the heavens, rushes earthward,
floods the streets.
                So much water is welcomed
            inside homes, a perfect stranger,
    who never complains about lodging,
a thirsty sibling up in the middle
    of the night. The moon washes
  its hands in the reflection of the vanquished.

If you build your house,
    build it so that it knows where to give, move
in rhythm with the ebb.
    Some call it a mad rush, like desire. Others
greet it with open arms,
              ease into it like baptism.
       What lures them is not the currents,
          but the possibility for travel.
     Surely birds know how to interpret
   the trees when they say "take flight."

The child who looks out beyond
    what the water and wind have taken, relishes
the no-school days.
          Farther beyond the fences,
      goats and pigs bleat and squeal.
   A fighting cock perches on a passing
log to preen its feathers. Everyone
  has learned to read their fate

in each drop of water, sheets of rain
           pelting the earth. When the time comes
they will sing to another season of departures.

Miami Beach

Waves rush in blue and clear,
    bathers bobbing like scabs on the surface,
the cafes and restaurants and bars
    all jammed with pink Germans
drinking beer, sun-bleached women
    with glasses of port in their meaty hands;
they don't know anything, these tourists
    from far away as Brazil, how in the early
1980s you could die in Miami Beach
    in an alley and not even the stench
of a rotting corpse would alarm people.
    On this beach only come the retirees, tired
Jews from New York, snow birds
    waiting for death to announce itself,
and they sit out on rattan rocking chairs,
    above them doomed pigeons crapping
on the window sills, and nobody minds.

They sink deep into the worn lobby sofas
    and vanish one at a time. Nobody
keeps count. On the street they coagulate
    on sidewalks, dragging metal walkers,
and canes. Old men with oxygen tanks,
    ex-smokers all, women in torn, stained
dresses—look at this place now,
    the developers have flushed out
the old and the sick, those who did not go,
    reversed mortgage their savings.
Gave way to the glitz and glamour,
    only the water remembers.
When all grows quiet, if you stand still

you can hear phlegmy coughs
echo in the hallways. Some of the dead
           linger, refusing to keep their mouths shut.

Night

I am sitting on a plastic chair
looking out at Biscayne Bay
toward the city of exile,

as most Cubans call Miami—
I catch my own reflection
on the door's sliding glass

that leads to the balcony, the eight-
story precipice ending down
at the pool where girls swim,

whisper boys' names in each
others' ears, pleasure giggles
rising in their throats the way

my own mortality surfaces
in my mind, gurgles there long enough
to sour and embitter my tongue.

These wicked thoughts of life
spent in the shallows,
my eyes reflected on the glass

like two shimmering orbs,
UFOs captured on grainy video,
a cartoon's bear-in-dark-cave

eyes, fireflies in my youth, jarred
and placed on my night stand,
in that distant paradise from which

I've been banished. We've all been there
since nobody can ever go home again.
What name do we give such sorrow?

Cuban Dream

I'm on the beach running after a red parasol, each time I get near,
a gust blows it down. It rolls over German & Italian tourists, tumbling,
kicking up sand into their drinks. They shout: "*Ragazzo*! *Achtung*!"
A red umbrella in the distance, a knotted-tendril medusa of all my dreams.
I run after it and step onto dead urchins. Needles spear my soles, prick deep.
Puas, as my father called these urchins, these pains, warning me to stay clear.
I leave blood tracks in the sand, beaded rubies of my passing.

A woman wants to know if I can help her reenact Ava Gardner's
Scene in *The Night of the Iguana*, the one with the two heavily-tanned boys
who sandwich the star in a sultry, so pre-called *lambada*. Pepe shakes his
maracas. The other, the nameless one, dances behind Ava, arms linked tight
about her waist. The forbidden dance. I say she's got the wrong time,
the wrong country.

The umbrella becomes a speck, a small dot my father's ghost plucks
out of the air and puts in his mouth. I've gone deaf. I don't even hear the waves.
Then suddenly I hear the roar of the surf breaking. I hear someone behind me
calling for another mojito. In the distance my father's ghost has become a raft
in a rough, angry sea. Women and children fall overboard, splash into the water.
Drown. Nobody notices. I turn to look behind me only to see a beach covered
in blue-white-red umbrellas and under their shades thousands of naked, flaccid
German women and men, their flabby skin turning lobster red. They are hungry
seals. One hobbles over to me and begins to gnaw at my shins. Her bite feels
like a clamping down of metal into flesh, the smashing of a finger under
a hammer's blow.

Paul Klee Visits Santiago de Cuba

after The Light and So Much Else

Beyond the "flying cities," the crosses, stripes,
this crop of dots hidden in the horizon,

you can count them and find your way back
anywhere, if you ask the sidewalk cracks,

they will show you the way, these little veins
and rivers on the walls. He came here

because he'd heard about a particular hue
of blue he'd heard a bird carried on its chest,

The Painted Bunting, see it with his own eyes,
this bird of paradise, but instead he fell in love

with the way light filled everything, the liquid
prism mirrored on the surface of the water.

A blue missing from his palette, luminous,
a tincture of diaphanous indigo, a straight

line so blue it drew breath from on-lookers.
Call it a whisp of the real Blues.

Those gathered on the shore gaze out
at the distance where they claimed to see

the fading lights of another shore, another country.
An artist mesmerized by a bird's spectral colors.

Dusk in the Tropics, a Parable of Light and Shadow

My father called it "*la boca del lobo.*"
      The wolf's mouth. The palm trees
lean closer to the earth, share
      secrets. White birds roost
on mangroves, become trash and paper,
      a word strangled between the Y
of branches. Blackbirds land
      on the electrical wires, roofs,
where water can't reach them.
      They chatter of plentiful food.
In a hut by the tourist traps,
      an old man sits, his legs crossed,
traces this arch of light, ascending
      into the horizon. The red he sees
are like his hands, his skin, what
      the dusk takes, it doesn't return.
Black, his soul rises skyward.
      When stars glitter-dust the night
sky, he can hear the voice of the drowning.
      Listen, you can hear them too
out beyond the buoys where the wolf
      opens its mouth one last time.

PART III

EXEGESIS

Repeating Island

after Antonio Benitez Rojo

My oldest daughter Alex brings me a map
        of the island of Cuba she's found in her history book.
                I am shaving and in the mirror in front of me
                        and the mirror behind me, this island

of my childhood repeats itself as many times
        as my eyes can look, and I think of the countless
                times a man, shaving, looks at a map of his country
                        multiply in the mirror, his daughter's annoyed

expression. I say, "Look how it goes, sweetie."
        She does not know what I am talking about, this
                endless repetition of exiles, caught
                        in the ad nauseam act of shaving, wiping

the slate clean, cutting themselves—all this blood shed
        in the traveling from one place to another. Sure,
                it is a simple act, this act of repetition, but clearly
                it shows us the way. There, on this mirror,

that one, the island rises from the depths of ocean,
        dresses itself in its most luscious green, it beckons
                us to return, the living and the dead, and you
                can imagine what the Tainos saw,

what Arawaks saw, what Siboneys saw, what Columbus himself
        must have seen, an island in the near distance, its lure
                a trace of green-blue tinge smudged in the horizon
                a mother, a son, on the verge of freedom.

Alma Profundis

for Liam, in pace requiescat

I cannot think of Bennington without you in it,
pulling up beside me in the car to save me from snow
and another fall (tropical birds simply cannot abide snow)—

"Get in," you said, your sunglasses a crow perched
low on the bridge of your nose . . . a scarf around your
neck. Always so dapper, Liam, haberdashery dapper fresh.

But this poem is really not about those cold nights
at Bennington College. It's about how your uncle hung
from the rafters, or how my cousin died by her own

hand, a slice of vein in the tub of warm soapy water.
The ghost of our jawless fathers by the campus pond,
2 a.m., night's pockets gutted of possibility and promise.

When there's nothing left for the heart to drum on,
let the dark silence be shattered by one last barbaric yawp,
one final struggle to swim home across 90 miles

of a treacherous Florida Straits, the place where I am now.
I am on a yacht a mere hairline away from my birthplace,
and these maternal waters are welcoming, sure, as if I could

simply drop into them and let the currents take me in,
down, deeper still until I can see and name the nameless dead,
balseros who've succumbed to the malaise of immortality,

much like you, me, the next graduate walking down the plank.

Poem on the Anniversary of Elián González's Return to Cuba

                    Nothing about the curb
or street in front of his uncle's
                    Westchester house

speaks of his playing,
                    his new bicycle,
his black Labrador puppy—

                    nothing in the sky
whispers the dreams the boy
                    tried to grasp on his cousin's

bed, a frothy wave lapping
                    at his chin, wiping worry
from his brow. A vision

of his mother's waving.

                    Nothing about the ebb
and flow of waves,
                    a remembrance of his body,

or hers—silence furrows
                    a yet-to-be-calmed sea.
If he counts the waves,

                    each crest carries with it,
this trace of memory:
                    a boy, his mother's

ghostly passing in the night,
                    no consolation of this quiet
act of erasure.

Recitative after G. de Chirico's *Les adieux* éternels

We are burying my father-in-law in the cemetery
on Calle Ocho in Miami, the one with the Cuban
flags, the mausoleum of ten-thousand martyrs

dead. The flowers spike the ground everywhere;
we weave among them, mortals awaiting the song
of the rooster. The sun glares off the pink roses,

the meaty ones paled by so much light; we walk
silent enshrouded in shadow. We are pallbearers,
my father-in-law's bones speak through the creaks

of the casket. Fernando, the man next to me, best
friend of the deceased cannot control himself so he
begins to hum Carlos Gardel's famous song: "*Adíos*

muchachos compañeros de mi vida . . ." The gaping
wound of earth awaits this body, and the next.
Flowering of the living, of the dying. In this light

Eliades Ochoa's words creep into my ear:
"*Los muertos van a la gloria y los vivos a bailar el son.*"
We dance on, ready to accept we are one with roses.

Gesture

My father sat at the kitchen table,
elbows on the table cloth, eyes still
as two nesting quails, he held

his hands in front of him and opened
each hand into a web of five scarred
fingers, then he touched their tips,

hand to hand. This was his leave-me-
alone-I'm-thinking gesture. We did.
My father's in the grave. My wife

claims she's caught me several times
doing my father's gesture. I tell her
though not to leave me alone, that

I am not thinking, not at all. Fire.
I am thinking of my father's fingers
as tongues of fire. He worked all day,

and sometimes at night: a bottle capper,
a pattern cutter, a slaughterer of animals.
I'm just a poet. But I can say, each tip

of my fingers is a river, a raft, every day
we swim home, go back to that place
where my father sat on the kitchen

table and looked out at another dying day.

The Mortician's Guayabera

It hangs behind the door, white like his hands,
after so much washing of bodies, flesh of pure

rapture. In the eyes of a dead child, a river
speaks of valleys, mountains, a scarf adrift

in the currents. In a dead man's mouth, a gift
of red words, a column of fire rising from cane

fields in the night. This man could be a father,
a son, or the Holy Trinity. A scar runs down his spine

toward the back of his left leg, a sienna canyon
caught between two cupped hands of earth.

It is a bird, this shirt of white, tropical humidity,
mist rising above sorghum fields in *el campo*, a *guajiro's*

garb, his suave style, ready for *decimas* and dance,
in the company of perfumed ladies, white bird,

egret, stork, dove rising there behind the door.
You would not know of its longing, it's passing.

In the night, when this man too used to silence
wears it out in the cool evening breeze, it glows.

It comes alive. A beacon to all those dying
for a proper burial at home. And if you return,

you will wear the plumage of birds on your back,
the color of brackish water in your eyes, salt or sugar

on your tongue, the sting of tears from such radiance.

The Pentagonies / *Las pentagonias de* Reinaldo Arenas

How many times did you, Reinaldo, were forced
to eat your own words? Piece of paper torn
from your journal, your entrails, feathers in your

mouth, rock-hard fists in your stomach. Each
time you spat fire back at those bastards. Five
times they took your novel, found it where you hid

it, burned it as though in fire your memory would
fail you, would not redeem you, and each time,
again, you wrote the same words, breathed them back

from the ashes of their violence and cruelty, and you
wrote them down time and again, these bright embers
ablaze on the vastness of your spirit, your gorgeous

soul and in the end, your words glow, hypnotic
light that exiles pray to, follow to arrive safely home
through distant fires of their own making—five novels

of wind, earth, water. What gives this land of impossibles
a gift like you? What brings your memory into the fold
of an eternal embrace. Your eyes opening finally liberated.

Ghazal of the Broken

for Dulce María Loynaz

Her shoes lay by the bed like fierce crows, hungry, crest-fallen,
one with its ear to the dark green carpet, the light shafted

through the open windows, curtains parted, outside a windless
day for the righteous, fertile seems the earth on such a day

when anything might be possible, a bed unmade, a framed
picture of night captured darkly on the canvas, a few paces

more and she would go naked out the window, her breasts
cut against the jagged glass, but she stands with her legs apart,

the light casting long shadows behind her, a cigarette burns
in her fingers and its smoke rises to burn in her eyes, solitude,

she thinks was invented for those who yearn for escape, after all
this and still no one knows her, sees her there in the room,

her elevator still works and that almost is all that matters,
and her garden. Her garden in the middle of a city in a country

dying daily for the lack of flowers, shadows, and poetry.

Wilfredo Lam at the Pantheon of the Paint Gods

Entre las sombras y tu boca, hay un pajaro tropical,
Between shadows and your mouth, a tropical bird

Flutters its wings, kicks up a centennial dust, ash,
que revoltea un siglo de polvo y ceniza,

that rains down upon trees in the jungle, prevents
la lluvia cae sobre los arboles, previene

the light from breaking through its thick curtain,
que la luz se asome atraves de una cortina gruesa

this curse of those who collect Lam's paintings,
take them out of Cuba, and when something terrible

happens to them, people ponder why, baffled
el que roba, muere entre comillas, la triztesa mata,

la melancholia de colores agonizantes: el rojo, verde,
violeta atormentado . . . between the canvas and paint,

two worlds, lovers caressing sun-warmed skin,
fingertips etched raw by grains of sand, *el ardor,*

la bestia en las entrañas, the moment of rapture,
how lines converge, melt into a vanishing point

that swallows everything into itself. *Las nubes*
un grito en las montañas. The painter eats his own

heart, colors drip from his eyes. *Los dioses*
de la pintura sonrién, sound their approval,

a cascading susurrus of a cicada's mating call.

Mariposas Negras: My Mother's Return to Cuba

When she arrived, she remembered the heat and splendor, the way a cloudless
sky made her eyes water, an ocean so verdant blue that sea birds stood out like
dots everywhere. Cuban Origami. The red dirt of her childhood games was still
there. In the little town of San Pablo, the cane fields all gone. Nothing left
of the house her parents built and made with their own hands. The gaping well
long covered by debris of countless hurricanes and history. Most of the fruit trees
replaced with *mala yerba* and jungle. The few people looked older, more weather-
beaten. What could she expect of so much time? Her mother and father both dead.
Not even the traces of graves nor floor foundations. Nothing. At night she listened
hard for the slightest sound of frog or cricket, the thick dust of memory now falling
over her body, like rain. The ash of the lives she lived in exile rebelling against erasure.

Orthography

My grandmother always strained
to hear the *sinsonte's* trill, this gun-
powder-chested canticle bird

in the blushed light of the afternoon
before dusk, a yearning to decipher
the individual notes, "*El estilo, niño,*"

mocking bird language stitched, stolen
from other birds—a court jester, he who
knew the ways of heart language,

or at least kept the count amused.
Sinsonte, el cantar de los cantores . . .
The way a bird whistles a thousand

variations to one need, one desire.
This lost portrait of a frail child
quieting to hear his own tender song.

Lotus Flower Balm, or Self Revelation with Praying Mantis Perched on My Finger

When sick, my mother melted
chicken fat in a teaspoon
over the stove, sprinkled a pinch

of salt in it, then brought it to me
to taste. The rest she smeared
and rubbed on my chest, placed

warm towels under my shirt.
My grandmother sat with me
in the room, afraid I inherited

my father's asthma—she read to me
about the Emperors in China,
the great mummies in Egypt,

about how in a Japanese garden,
the world kissed on the petals
of the lotus flower, these open

hands afloat on the shimmer
of koi-infested ponds, and soon
you close your eyes and dream

of a praying mantis who whispers
lucky knowledge of green leaves,
gardenia blossom on its breath—

chest heat, fire in the hands, snow
falling on an open mind—a child
levitating toward a billowed mosquito

netting, his life blown to smithereens.

Claritas

for Robert Bly

I plunge my fists into the moist earth,
branches of a fallen man, mildew green

teeth gnawing at the impossibility of love,
ancient child of rumination, criss crossed

star-gazers lost in the blush of a serpentine
moon. To see clearly, a man must chew

his own heart; to hear seismic songs,
he must not catch up to his long shadow.

Water reflects only the kind of truth,
this thin veneer of the lost and hopeless.

My father said it best when he said:
"One day you will turn to dust, crumble

like the greatest of monuments, the earth
will embrace you in your sad corruption."

The body is a vessel, sure, rudderless,
cutting through time and air, leaving

evidence of its passing on the backs
of leaves. My fists sprout gardenias

as white as my tongue, as gorgeous
as my moonlit skin, this fire-hue of clarity.

Fantomas, Master of Disguise

In the mid 60s, after the Revolution,
the movie trucks came to the suburbs
in Havana on Saturday nights to show

foreign films dubbed in Spanish.
When the film glitched or flickered
or the sound went off, people grew

restless and started to boo, fights
broke out, food got thrown on the pull-
down screen on the side of the truck,

and my father brought me to watch
this magic of film, car chases, caravels
lost at sea, camels traversing the Egyptian

desert, and the *Fantomas* films,
about a master of disguises and masks
who was his own man, an evil genius,

half villain, half Robin Hood.
The British Intelligence is always after
him, but he gets away or hides,

via the *disfrazes,* as my father called
them, and Fantomas got away in a white
car, which also traveled flew like a plane,

and these films became big hits
in our neighborhood, and until they
made adults not want to get up to work

voluntarily on Sundays, picking tomatoes,
cabbages and corn, and the films stopped
coming, and slowly people gravitated

toward the same corner every Saturday
night, the men talking soft, the women
fanning their faces with newspaper.

The children played hide-and-seek,
pretended to be like Fantomas, master spy
who nobody could catch, and we disappeared

indeed as families started leaving the country,
entire families gone by morning, some to Spain,
others to the United States, many never to return.

At night I dreamt of Fantoma's white car,
pulling up to the front of our house, me and my
parents getting in it, my father touching the dials

on the dashboard, these gadgets that only Fantomas
know how they worked, the car going under water.
I could see the coral reef, schools of fish darting

all around, and I would close my eyes
and wake up in this land of constant vanishers.

Exegesis

I once took a Southern Literature class at LSU
from Louis Simpson, the imminent Southern scholar,
      and we talked about mostly, the Agrarians,

the Fugitives, and Robert Penn Warren's novel
All the King's Men, which I read for the first time
      and loved, and found out too that it had loaned

it's title to *All the President's Men,* the Watergate
bible. Watergate was important to me because
      I arrived in the United States as an immigrant

right then in 1974, and since I didn't yet speak
a word of English, it wasn't until college that I
      understood that it had been the ugliest

of political nightmares for this country.
I kept thinking of "water" and "gates," the way
      people are kept out, the way I think

of cages now, but that's another story.
I like to translate words from English to Spanish,
      and then back for the "*mantequilla*"

in the "*mosca*" which becomes *butterfly.*
I remembered the joke the old professor imparted
      upon us about "Red's"—that's what

he called Mr. Penn Warren, or rather the time
his Fugitive poet friends had nicknamed him—
      being asked about what he taught,

and someone hearing "poultry" instead of "poetry."
And Penn Warren making a life-long joke of it.
So, I'm in class and I kept listening

to other students talking about "exit Jesus"
this and "exit Jesus" that, and I look through the text
trying to figure out what, if anything,

Jesus had to do with our reading, with this class,
so I kept thinking religion and its effects on Southern
Literature and I saw the connection when we

begun to read McCarthy's *Child of God*, and how
vicious man can be, but my classmates kept saying the
word over and over, until the day I'd had enough,

confused beyond belief about Jesus and Southern
Literature, I raised my hand and asked: "What does
Jesus have anything to do with any of this?"

Professor Simpson smiled, then started laughing,
then the rest of the class joined in. "Look it up,
Mr. Suárez," he said. "You might learn

something new one day." It wasn't until years
later that looking up the word "excavation," that I
turned the pages of the dictionary and found

"exegesis." It glowed up at me, and I read it means
"to explain the text," and it made me smile because
in schools words become fashionable, cool.

I've been explaining my life away via texts
that most students could care less about, and I say,
listen, watch carefully for there he goes,

there goes Jesus exiting now.

PART IV

HYPER~
GRAPHIA

Bad Sons Anonymous

At this year's convention
we gather to pay homage
to our fathers, responsible
men who worked hard:

laborers, stone cutters, welders,
carpenters—blue collar all,
men who raged, stormed
their anger through the house,

our mothers couldn't manage,
swept with brooms the debris
of broken things, in silence
they took it out on us, belts

in hand, we stood there, cried,
long days turned to long nights,
our fathers, mothers, damages
done, we, as their only sons,

remember. We, as bad sons,
pay them back, one mirror held
up to another, an infinity
of their gnarled faces, red-blue-fire

what has become lost in all of us.

My Father, the Arsonist

Some men live on the yolk of raw eggs
Bled into a shot of vermouth

     in my father's mouth

a fist of coal-black cinders, smouldered
at the end of a hard day's work;

     his hands

singed into gnarled raven claws. He spoke
in riddles with the wisdom of the dead,

     brokered my life

with adages he'd heard dragged
across the barren field of childhood,

dead leaves, animals to slaughter:
his dreams, his fortune, his optimism . . .

     At home he stripped

naked in the laundry room,
his smouldering clothes in a pile.

I read bad news in the wisps of smoke,
Saw the devil in repose, rolling himself

     an Habano,

licked it smooth with his forked tongue.
My father dreamt of fires, tossed/turned

in flame.

An insomniac he roamed the dark
By the beam through slit eyes. No moon,

no shadows. I once watched

him cough up molten lava during years
he worked a the foundry, his skin already

singed and riddled

with bruises, cuts, scabs . . . my mother
rubbed him down with salve, her own

ointment concoction—

dripped chamomile tea into the back
of his swollen, raw throat. I grew up

as my father's translator

between the sun and the scorched earth,
watched the heat waver in his wake.

My father danced

brimstone over the charred lip of horizon.
I called out to him to stop.

I could not extinguish his name
Emblazoned there in my darkest path.

The Beautiful Light

Most of the world is disappearing.
One car at a time, one person.

My daughter's endocrinologist
says it's a fresh canvas every hundred

years, a new slate that continues
to repeat itself, yellowing all along.

A slow demise and sinuous flaccidity
to the flesh. Metal rusts. Organic

material decays. We make time cringe
at will, but time doesn't seem to even

want to linger in this pocket of marsh
where a terrapin's snout disturbs a froth

of duckweed and algae. Insects freeze
inside the pages of an ancient book.

It's daylight savings again, here comes
that light that casts a shadow on the porch.

A bloody cardinal files its complaint
to the sun that the squirrels hoard

all the seed in the broken bird feeder.
On a desolate highway, a roof caves

in at the abandoned motel. A tile crushes
the rat. A nest of wasps is torn asunder.

That buzzing you hear is the light
fighting back its inability to remember

we'd been here in this same room
watching Hopper paint the billowed

curtain. Outside the clouds drag themselves
across the landscape again. They speak

a ruckus in eternal and yet momentary
sameness. They will be back tomorrow, right?

Bloodlines

My father's been long gone,
down some dusty road in Cuba,
always v a n i s h i n g . . .

On the good days I think it a trick
of perspective, all the crap I learned
in art school . . . scattering dirt

out of one pocket and heirloom
tomato seeds out the other, he goes.
I am following as best as I could

through these last few years,
my hair as plentiful and thick
as his was, although salted now.

My mother reminds me I have not
paid my respects at the cemetery
where a few times a year she tends

his plot, this green yawn of a mouth
he inhabits. Bloodclots, massive coronary,
the breadcrumbs I've been tracking

down this winding road, staving off
his bitterness derived from eternal exile.
My father the simple man, a quiet bird

huddled in the shade of a mango tree,
his eyes dark as caverns, waiting
for the sun to go down over the hills

so he can move on. My father sings
a bluesy *decima*, and I hear
the cadence of his walk, one boot

in front of the other, kicking up dust
into my eyes, my mouth. A bucket
dangles in a dry well, a faint hiss

of insects in the air . . . this metronome
of how a son follows his father
into that azure valley

where everything
keeps sprouting, growing,
returning to the same

earth that welcomes us home.

El Rio (Mississippi)

Whenever I cross the Mississippi in Baton Rouge
on my motorcycle I feel the wheels wiggle and slide

against the iron grating at the dead center of the bridge
and I think about the first time dawn found me on the levee

waking from a night of drunkenness and debauchery,
a New Orleans girlfriend still wrapped in the blanket

next to me and I wonder how we meandered, quite often
to and from this river. In Spanish river means *rio*

like the Havana Almendares where my father took me
fishing. He was a young man and I, his only son, stood

by as he caught nothing. Time and again he tugged
on the line and pretended he'd caught something just to see

the excitement in my eyes, my jaw slacking open.
All of this in the flash of the polluted chocolate waters

rolling way underneath the wheels of my bike.
Polluted, somber, this river takes all it's given.

Like the life we waste, one love at a time. Well spent,
on fire, hopefully. In the air you can taste the mud

the sulphur of the refineries bleaching into its waters.
This mighty river is in fact fighting their poisoning.

The fish glow phosphorescent in the night. Rebirth
a distant promise somewhere down in the Gulf.

Barges, like broken teeth, cut the river, make it bleed
slick and broken in oil. Sometimes what kills you

will make you stronger, my father often said. Riverside,
soul food up ahead and we hunger for the slaw & jambalaya

a cold bottle of Abita to wash it all down. The river
courses right on through our days and nights, still glowing.

Detroit Low-Down Canto

Cracked bells clamor in the ripening hour,
tar-feather crows droop on sagging wires
a knotted spool unraveled years ago
greedy pavement cracks vein toward a dried-

up heart, molten and smithed down to a hard
gnarled fist, rust consumes the last bit of steel,
hear the wind whistle that shift-change tune
from long ago: cheaper faster, cheaper faster,

my friend called it, the choo-choo train
of capitalism chugs to a dead stop.
Where are the suits now? Those fuckers
devoid of redemption with their black

and bitter tongues? Idealess, they've gone
off to plunder the next city, plunge their wicked
divining rods into the earth. Here: only the dust
knows the truth, and sparrows wasted

from the hunger curl into desiccated puffs.
One by one they freeze in empty nests in corrugated
tin crevices. Nobody knows they are there,
shriveled and hollowed-bone. Elsewhere a last

car drives on the longest highway into oblivion.
Hear the pin drop, a last hammer kissing an anvil.
What drives us to ruin isn't greed, nor indifference,
it's how easily we choke on broken promises.

Detroit, lost city, needs to feed on the blood
of drawn-and-quartered politicos. Round them up
and gut them in the town square, let them see
the sun rising once again through lidless eyes.

Erasure

Hangman, hangman, hold it a little while,
I think I see my friends coming, riding many a mile.
—Led Zeppelin

The mirrors in the restaurant of exile shattered today.

My father's remains recompose, his heart pumps & flutters

as he joins the dead digging themselves out of countless graves.

No more dancing. No more singing. The streets change

names. The airplane that brought us propels itself

in reverse, a sky monster choking on its own sooty smoke.

Hazy blood point of perspective diminishing in the distance.

Who fights oblivion to win? Who wants history to absolve them?

We did not belong here, nor will we exist here much longer.

The Magic City crumbles to rubble first, then sand, then dust.

In the straits waves regurgitate the many who drown.

Nobody remembers their names or stories, but they float back

beyond the detritus and flotsam. The asphyxiated walk backward

in camara lenta, long enough for the tropical light to bring back color to their gaunt faces, and reed-hollowed bodies. The sun counterfits

its purpose. The island frees itself long enough to enjoy a last cafecito.

In 1962 a man holds his son for the first time, a moist seedling

who will lose itself into a dark and sterile earth. This couple marry

and move to a ravaged city to coil back through impossible

beginnings in 1959—the year a murder of crows ravaged the harvest.

Before that came the hurricanes, the Spanish raping the Tainos.

And even before that the first coconut and the first palm. Lava. Earth.

The sand retreating below the ocean, cooling and burning itself out.

Who were we? What became of us? Those marks we left in the wake

of all this vanishing taking place in another place where the mirrors

are black or covered with stained bed sheets and old rags. Cracked, we

do not recognize ourselves in the cobwebs of that rubble we called home.

Let Us Refresh (Alvarez Guedes's Ascension into Comedy Heaven)

The nose gave you away, that charming smile
which demonstrated your mind ran fifteen blocks
ahead of your audience. The joke's the thing:
your timing Swiss clockwork and perfect.

My father listened to you all his years in exile,
and when I inherited all those numbered LPs,
I'd listen to them late at night when I thought
I'd forget how to laugh in Spanish. *Hay que refrescar!*

Clearly a life-long philosophy for everyone here
in those dark and empty corners we call *El Asilo*.
Life is too short, right? And too full of shit.
Te cagas en la mierda! *Me cago, nos cagamos*

of laughter, in laughter, that vessel that kept hair
on your face. Your infamous broom mustache,
those picaro eyes, Alvarez. You killed us time
and again with your humor. Laughter's the salve,

you did not have to say it. You lived it.
I listened to your GUANTANAMERA renditions
every day on the radio, now silent and static.
Guedes, you rascal, you've been taken from us.

The sky everywhere is crisp and the air crackles
as fast as your punchlines fill these Miami streets.
Prince of Making Sense, King of Displacement . . .
Let the rains cleanse this city, *Sigues refrescando*!

Poem on the 10th Anniversary of Janet Jackson's Nipple

I hope the Transylvanian SEACROWS beat the Lunar BRONCHITIS.
They say syphilis makes you lose your mind, later, so they say . . .

I threw out my back this morning looking up syphilis in the medical
dictionary, one heavy mother of a book. Looked up sciatica as well.

Those early Greeks sure had time on their hands. At least the Romans
knew how to have fun, one lion vs Christian at a time.

Do I need more catheters? I better put in another order. I truck
goods from State to State, and this beats bathroom pit stops.

Too much foie gras consumption has caused my fatty liver.
I am sleeping with my proctologist, a man who also knows how

to laugh when he hears a good how-many-does-it-take-to joke.
Today I gave nothing at church, found nothing but lint in my heart.

Someone attempted to kill the previous president and failed. Darn.
My youngest daughter wants to be a doctor so she can cure

her father's ADHD. Perhaps a mallet will work. Or the incessant
song of two crickets in each ear. Nudity in movies is over rated.

My nipples are dark and hairy, crowned by a Mona Lisa of moles.
I am not a fan of porcelain bathtubs, so I have to wear flip-flops.

Something about my father taking me to the public bathrooms
at the beach—all that yellow, sludge sand between my toes . . .

Once the only thing that came between Brooke Shields and her
Calvin Klein's were a couple of layers of really viscous Valvoline oil.

Bob Dylan drives a new Cadillac, that piece of shit—the car, not BD.
Isn't football played with the feet? The ball is oblong because

it is female. Fumble? Again. Pass the gene-engineered chips, please.
Look, a streaker on the field. I LOVE YOU, NIKE!

Harry Dean Stanton Is Dying

> The sun is dying out.
> —Harry Dean Stanton, from
> *Harry Dean Stanton: Partly Fiction*

See it in the crow-black eyes, the stubble
and the way his lids sag as he belts out

the next sad song. Jack Nicholson's gone
for good, an empty husk at the bottom

of the push cart. My daughter Skypes
from the Cancer Ward in a Guatemalan

Children's Hospital, something about a boy
named Lester who has no parents, no relatives.

Lester in a cancer-riddled body, only a matter
of time before the next Mexican ranchera comes on.

Lester who misses his roommate who's gone
for specialized treatment in the United States,

Lester of the non-sequiturs: a man walking
out of a soccer stadium in the middle of the jungle

in Manaus, takes off his clothes and plunges
into the moonlit river only to become the fish

who forgot the upstream way home. Lester who
is dying and who's become the ticking in my clock.

Harry Dean says Rebecca De Mornay broke
his heart. Now Lester has mine in his mouth

and when he yawns, you can see the black moths
stuck to the cavernous palate. Who will save

Harry Dean from dying? Who will save Lester
from erasure and the fact that only my daughter

and I (now) will speak his name out of the shadows.
Come, Lester, the sun is dying, but not so soon.

Look out the window at the silvering river and the man
swimming upstream who glistens and shimmers

and takes his next deep breath, don't stop singing.

The Lion Head Belt Buckle

My father bought it for me as a gift in the Madrid *rastro*
near where we lived, new immigrants from Cuba.

The eyes and mane carved deep into the metal, the tip of the nose
already thin with the blush of wear. My mother found a brown

leather strap and made it into a belt with enough slack and holes
to see me wearing it in Los Angeles where we landed next.

My father worked at *Los Dos Toros*, a meat market run by Papito,
A heavy-set man with a quick smile and when I would visit

the market after school to wait for my father to bring me home,
Papito always talked to me about baseball and his favorite

Cincinnati Reds players. It was there one of his employees,
a skinny man with deep set eyes and crow-feather black

hair would stop me in the narrow hallway by the produce tables
and grab the belt buckle and praise it. All along passing his hand

over my penis. "You are strong," he would whisper, "like this lion."
I would recoil from his touch and move away back to the front

where Papito would ask me about what bases I intended
to play next season on *Los Cubanitos* team. I never told my father,

or anyone, but the afternoon I showed up and the Fire Department
and police and ambulances huddled in the alleyway behind

Los Dos Toros, I knew something terrible had happened. Some
other kid had uttered the man's groping and insisting on a kiss

in the *almacén,* the darkened storage room pass the meat locker.
And another father had taken matters into his own hands.

But instead I found my father hosing the back door entrance,
washing the blood down to the alleyway. He told me to wait for him

in the car. The paramedics rolled out Papito, shot and dead on a stretcher,
victim of a hold up. The dark Cuban man who'd felt me up time

and again stood in the shade of a tree weeping and kicking the dirt
with blood encrusted shoes. I found out later he was the one who

slammed the assailant against the wall, and beat him unconscious.
Fuerte como un leon. The words fluttered like cow birds in the back

of my mind. Scattershot and ringing like the violence among the men.

Alba Written at Bennington College

No caw of roosters to greet the pale snow here,
nothing stirs at this hour, not even the mice
buried deep in the ice. I stop to piss by a tree

but notice that a dog has beaten me to the spot,
a yellow smear near the tree's trunk. I hate how
snow crunches under my boots. My crow hands

nested in my pockets. My breath ghosts every word
I want to utter in name of such loneliness, such magic,
but my mouth is merely a slit through which enough

air passes inside my lungs. On my way home
in this white world where everything seems to forget
the idea of green, my memory becomes a cardinal

shooting across the snow like a drop of blood.

Hypergraphia

The monster rises from nocturnal slumber
to sit at his writing table, he is a real beast

with overgrown hair, bushy eyebrows,
feet swollen from the daily jog—anything

to keep from writing, so the doctor ordered,
but at night he cannot help it. He hears

the pencil and paper calling, sand wisped
into glass, water dripping in the toilet.

He's opted for the handcuff cure, the chains
around his arms, this straight jacket method

to keep his arms from even gesturing what
he means. When he hears the line by Bly:

"A word shows up at your door . . . "
Multitudes of them awaiting his return

from the subconscious and dreams of caverns
in Southeaster Cambodia, this palace of moss.

He drinks decaf, sits on his hands, bites
his tongue, his lips, worlds all the time welling

up in his throat. Fingers itch. If only he were
a thorn bird, sing once and plunge to the death

against a dagger. Even better, saw off his fingers,
or better still, hack off his arms, but he's afraid

even then they'd coil like eels around his ankles,
take hold, not release him until he writes down

this next word—of course, there's the self-inflicted
lobotomy, but he doesn't have the *cojones*, ño.

ACKNOWLEDGMENTS

Grateful acknowledgment is made to the editors and publishers of the following reviews and journals where some of these poems first appeared, sometimes in slightly different form:

> *ACM, Quarter After Eight, ON THE BUS, Limestone, Iodine Poetry Journal, Miramar, New Delta Review, Grist 7, Thorny Locust, Mobious, Monarch Review, Mas Tequila Review, Potomac Review, South Florida Poetry Review, Caribbean Writer, Chariton Review, Comstock Review, Controlled Burn, Crab Orchard Review, Crazyhorse, Dalhousie Review, Florida Review, Grain* (Canada), *Imago* (Australia), *International Poetry Review, Literary Review, Louisiana Literature, Many Mountains Moving, James Dickey Review, Marlboro Review, New England Review, New Orleans Review, Ontario Review, Other Poetry* (England), *Oxford Magazine, Paris/Atlantic* (France), *Peer Poetry Review* (England), *Pleiades, Ploughshares, Poet Lore, Prairie Schooner, Quarterly West, Queen's Quarterly* (Canada), *River Styx, Sow's Ear Poetry Review, Dos Passos Review, Tampa Review, 2 Bridges Review, Virginia Quarterly Review, Washington Square, Westview, Willow Review,* and *Windsor Review* (Canada).

"Benediction for a Caribbean Moon" first appeared in *The Night's Magician: Poems about the Moon,* edited y Philip C. Kolin and Sue Brannan Walker, published by Negative Capability Press, Alabama, 2018, page 89.

"Harry Dean Stanton Is Dying" appeared in *Reel Verse: Poems about Movies,* edited by Harold Schechter and Michael Waters, published by Everyman's Library Pocket Poets, Alfred A. Knopf, New York, 2019, pages 119–20.

Some of the poems in the "Hypergraphia" part of this book are part of chapbook by the same title, published in a limited edition by Hysterical Books, 2019.

For the fresh eyes and words of encouragement, I would like to thank in no particular order: Adrian C. Louis, Mark Doty, Bruce Weigl, Ed Ochester, Christopher Buckley, Judith Vollmer, Denise Duhamel, Charles Harper Webb, Liam Rector, E. Ethelbert Miller, and Richard Blanco. I would also like to thank all of my colleagues at Bennington College for the many years of friendship and support.

Fifteen years have passed during the creation and revising of this book and the one constant has been the love and emotional stability of my wife and family, in particular my two daughters.